Original title:
Twinkle Time and Sleepy Rhymes

Copyright © 2024 Creative Arts Management OÜ
All rights reserved.

Author: Henry Beaumont
ISBN HARDBACK: 978-9916-90-392-6
ISBN PAPERBACK: 978-9916-90-393-3

The Comfort of Painted Stars

In the silence of the night,
Stars hang like dreams in flight.
Each twinkle whispers a tale,
Of gentle winds and moonlit sail.

Above the world, they softly gleam,
Filling hearts with hope and dream.
A canvas stitched with silver light,
Guiding lost souls through the night.

Slumbering in Celestial Fields

In fields where whispers weave and play,
Celestial blooms greet the day.
Gentle waves of stardust flow,
Cradling secrets that we sow.

The soft embrace of twilight's song,
Lulls weary hearts to rest along.
As shadows dance with the silent breeze,
While dreams awaken under trees.

Chasing Shadows at Dusk

As daylight fades and shadows grow,
We chase the dusk with hearts aglow.
Whispers of twilight softly call,
Guiding our steps, lest we fall.

The world transforms in fading light,
Colors blend, a wondrous sight.
In every corner, magic stirs,
As night unveils the dreams of hers.

Gentle Breezes and Pillow Dreams

Gentle breezes drift and sway,
Carrying whispers of the day.
Pillows cradle thoughts anew,
As night unfolds a tranquil view.

In soft embrace, we find our peace,
Where worries fade and tensions cease.
Wrapped in warmth, we float and glide,
In dreamland's arms, we safely hide.

Pastel Skies and Midnight Sighs

Pastel hues brushed on the dawn,
Whispers of dreams linger on.
Clouds dance softly in the light,
Promises bloom, hearts take flight.

Golden rays peek through the gray,
Chasing the shadows far away.
In twilight's embrace, we find peace,
As the day's worries gently cease.

Stars awaken, a twinkling show,
Mapping tales of love below.
In midnight's sigh, secrets play,
Guiding the night until the day.

Fables of the Cloudy Night

A tapestry woven of dreams and chance,
Fables unfurl in a moonlit dance.
Softly the clouds tell tales anew,
Of secret wishes, of hearts so true.

The night sky whispers in tones so sweet,
Where lost souls gather, their journeys meet.
With every star, a story spins,
Of laughter, of love, of loss, and wins.

Echoes of laughter drift through the air,
Illuminated paths, a light to share.
In the embrace of shadows, we find,
The magic that binds both heart and mind.

Heavenly Capsules of Serenity

In the stillness of the night,
Capsules of calm take flight.
Gentle breezes weave through trees,
Singing soft songs with perfect ease.

Moonbeams shimmer on tranquil seas,
Carrying whispers on the breeze.
Each pulse of time, a treasure rare,
A moment cradled, light as air.

Journey through twilight, a serene quest,
Where silence envelops, hearts find rest.
In starlit chambers, dreams unfold,
In heavenly whispers, stories told.

Tales of the Cozy Cosmos

Under a blanket of stars so bright,
The cosmos cradles the gentle night.
Each twinkle speaks of ancient lore,
Of cozy moments, and so much more.

In the arms of the universe, we lay,
Drifting through dreams, night turns to day.
With every heartbeat, the galaxies show,
The warmth of connection, the love that we know.

Softly the night wraps us in its cloth,
A tapestry woven, no paths to swath.
In this embrace, we find our home,
Tales of the cosmos, we're never alone.

Sleepy Shores of Imagination

Waves of dreams softly crash,
Whispering secrets to the night.
Sands of thought gently dance,
Under the moon's silver light.

Drifting ships of fantasy,
Sail on the sea of the mind.
Anchored in sweet reverie,
Where time is tender and kind.

Clouds of cotton float above,
Painting stories in the sky.
Hearts find solace in their love,
As the stars begin to sigh.

Stars in My Eyes

Twinkling lights in velvet skies,
Guide my dreams where wonders flow.
I see magic in your eyes,
A dance of galaxies aglow.

Whispers soft like evening breeze,
Carry wishes on their flight.
Wrapped in warmth and gentle ease,
The universe feels just right.

With each blink, new worlds appear,
Infinite tales to explore.
In this calm, I have no fear,
As I wander evermore.

The Silent Song of Slumber

Gentle lullabies surround,
In the quiet of the night.
Resting where peace can be found,
Wrapped in dreams of soft delight.

Hushed whispers of the moon,
Singing softly to my heart.
Every note a perfect tune,
As the night begins to start.

Drifting on a velvet cloud,
Peaceful shadows sway and weave.
In this moment, dreams are proud,
Telling tales that we believe.

Midnight Dreams in Bloom

In the garden of the night,
Dreams awaken, softly bloom.
Petals glisten in the light,
Perfumed whispers fill the room.

Stars are scattered like sweet seeds,
Planting joy within my soul.
Each thought nurtures gentle needs,
Growing quiet, growing whole.

Close your eyes and drift away,
Let the dreams take you apart.
In this moment, lost but gay,
Feel the rhythm of your heart.

Chronicles of Starlit Sleep

In the hush of night, whispers weave,
Tales of dreams that softly cleave.
Stars like lanterns flicker bright,
Guiding souls through endless night.

Moonlight drapes the world in grace,
Casting shadows, leaving trace.
Crickets sing a lullaby,
As the echoes slowly die.

Resting minds in gentle loops,
Floating high on silver swoops.
Each moment, twilight's gift,
In slumber's care, our spirits lift.

Awakened by the morning's glow,
Memories of night bestow.
Chronicles in dreams we keep,
Valleys wide of starlit sleep.

Echoes of the Dusk

As the sun bids soft adieu,
Night unveils a deepened hue.
Whispers dance on evening's breath,
Carrying tales of love and death.

Leaves sigh softly in the dark,
Nature's heartbeat, quiet spark.
Lost in thoughts of days gone by,
The shadows stretch, then gently sigh.

Stars awake in velvet skies,
Filling hearts with secret lies.
Keeping watch on dreams unspun,
Until the rise of morning sun.

In the dusk's embrace we find,
Echoes of the night unwind.
Holding close the fading light,
Nurtured by the peace of night.

Enchanted Dreams Await

Beneath the stars, a path unfolds,
Whispers of the night retold.
In the stillness, dreams take flight,
Guided by the moon's soft light.

Faeries dance on silver beams,
Woven into hopeful dreams.
Magic lingers in the air,
Waiting for a heart to dare.

With each breath, the world transcends,
In the night, the spirit bends.
Chasing shadows, losing sleep,
Through enchanted realms we leap.

Morning comes with gentle rain,
Washing off the night's refrain.
In our hearts, the dreams will stay,
Enchanted visions lead the way.

Laidback Starlight

Under the stars, the night is still,
Each moment whispers, soft and chill.
Laidback dreams in twilight's glow,
Drifting where the breezes blow.

Time meanders, slow and sweet,
Every heartbeat, a gentle beat.
Clouds of silver float so near,
Encasing dreams we hold so dear.

Night unfolds a canvas wide,
Where wanderers of starlight glide.
With every sigh, the world feels right,
In the ease of laidback night.

As dawn approaches, shadows fade,
Yet memories of night are made.
Holding close, we softly sigh,
Laidback starlight in our eye.

A Sleepy Voyage to Starlit Shores

The moonlight whispers soft and low,
As gentle waves begin to flow.
A sleepy breeze drifts through the night,
Guiding dreams on wings of light.

Stars twinkle in a velvet sea,
A serenade for you and me.
With every lull, our hearts afloat,
We journey on a velvet boat.

Whispers of fate paint the skies,
As we chase the dreams that rise.
From distant shores we long to find,
A world where hearts and souls unwind.

In this slumber's sweet embrace,
We sail to a magical place.
Beneath the stars' enchanting glow,
The starlit shores begin to show.

Shadows Swaying to the Rhythm of Night

Beneath the silver moon's embrace,
Shadows dance in a silent grace.
Whispers glide on winds so light,
Swaying softly through the night.

Branches twist with secrets old,
While stories of the dark unfold.
The stars align in cosmic song,
Inviting dreams to drift along.

Crickets chirp a lullaby sweet,
Echoes of the night discreet.
The rhythm beats in nature's heart,
As shadows twirl and weave their art.

In the stillness, magic breathes,
Among the leaves, the night believes.
Each shadow moves in perfect rhyme,
To the timeless dance of night-time.

Nightfall's Gentle Hand and Dreamer's Flight

As dusk descends, the world turns bright,
Nightfall's hand brings dreams to light.
Softly wrapped in starry sheets,
The whispering wind gently greets.

With hearts aloft, we rise and soar,
Into the night, we long for more.
Magic beckons, we take the leap,
Across the skies, our spirits sweep.

Visions dance on clouds of dreams,
Bathed in silver, the moonlight gleams.
Time stands still, the world is wide,
In dreams we trust, we will abide.

Through cosmic gates, our souls entwined,
In realms where love and hope align.
Night's gentle hand, a guiding light,
Awakens dreams that take their flight.

Echoes of Serenity through the Starlit Veil

In the hush of night, serenity flows,
Underneath the starlit shows.
Whispers of the cosmos bright,
Caress our hearts, igniting light.

The velvet sky, a canvas wide,
Holds echoes where our dreams reside.
With every twinkle, stories weave,
A tapestry in which we believe.

Moments linger, sweet and rare,
Captured softly in the air.
Through the veil of stars above,
We find a world of peace and love.

So let us listen to the night,
To echoes of serenity's light.
Together we shall drift away,
In starlit dreams, forever stay.

The Quietude of Dreaming Dawn

In the hush of early light,
Soft whispers play,
Gentle beams a-frolic,
As night slips away.

Colors blend in silence,
A canvas aglow,
Hopeful hearts awaken,
While the night breezes blow.

Birds sing sweetly breaking,
The stillness of dreams,
Nature's joyful calling,
In harmonious themes.

With every eager flutter,
Life begins anew,
The quietude of morning,
A world fresh and true.

Moonbeam Murmurs and Restful Rhymes

Silver light in shadows,
Gently wraps the ground,
Whispers of the nighttime,
A soft, soothing sound.

Moonbeams dance like echoes,
Across the tranquil sea,
A lullaby of silver,
In perfect harmony.

Stars twinkle and shimmer,
Their secrets left untold,
Restful rhymes in starlight,
As the night unfolds.

In this serene embrace,
Dreams drift and unwind,
With moonbeam murmurs echoing,
A solace we can find.

Stars that Stitch the Fabric of Night

In a tapestry of darkness,
Stars begin to weave,
Threads of light and shadow,
In patterns we believe.

Each star a whispered secret,
A spark in the expanse,
Connecting distant stories,
In a timeless dance.

Their glow ignites the silence,
A symphony so bright,
Binding the night together,
In a cloak of pure light.

They twinkle with intention,
Guiding souls that roam,
Stars that stitch the fabric,
Of the night's vast dome.

Hushed Echoes of Twilight's Grace

As day gives way to slumber,
Hues of dusk arrive,
Whispers in the twilight,
Where dreams come alive.

Softly shades are blending,
A palette, rich and wide,
Hushed echoes of the evening,
As stars begin to glide.

Crickets chirp their symphony,
A serenade so sweet,
Nature sings her bedtime song,
In rhythms slow and neat.

With twilight's gentle presence,
Rest comes without haste,
In the depths of darkness,
We find our perfect grace.

Starlit Reveries

In the night where shadows play,
Stars whisper secrets softly,
Dreams dance upon silver beams,
Embracing the cosmic sea.

Underneath the moon's embrace,
Time slips through like golden sands,
We wander through starlit trails,
Hand in hand, in dreamland's hands.

Weaver's Night

Threads of twilight weave the sky,
An artist's brush paints nighttime hues,
With every stitch a wish is sewn,
Linking hearts with glittering views.

In the quiet, patterns form,
Stories told in threads of light,
Each heartbeat echoes gently,
In the weaver's calming night.

The Tranquil Song of Fading Day

Whispers of the evening glow,
A lullaby of soft goodbye,
Each note drips like honeydew,
As colors blend in twilight's sigh.

The sun bows low, a gentle kiss,
On horizons painted red,
The tranquil song fills the air,
As dreams begin to thread.

Slumbering Garden of Cosmic Blush

In gardens where the starlight blooms,
Petals kiss the evening air,
Dreams nestle in the fragrant night,
Wrapped in the cosmos' care.

Softly whispering to the stars,
The moonlight joins the silent dance,
In the slumbering garden's heart,
Dreamers sway in a trance.

Dreams that Drift in the Cool Night Air

Floating softly on the breeze,
Whispers sweet as night unfolds,
Dreams drift in a cool embrace,
Stories waiting to be told.

The nightingale sings her song,
Echoing through moonlit glades,
While dreams that drift like feathered clouds,
Gracefully weave the night's cascades.

Nighttime's Caress

The moon whispers soft to the trees,
In shadows where whispers linger and tease.
Stars blink like dreams in the dark,
A gentle embrace where silence sparks.

Night's breath is cool, a tender sigh,
Cradling the world as the day says goodbye.
Mellowed edges blur into the night,
Painting the sky with a shimmery light.

Crickets weave songs in the breeze,
Nature's lullaby, a calming ease.
In this stillness, hearts gently yield,
To the soothing balm of night's quiet field.

Under the cloak of the velvet sky,
Dreams take flight, like birds they fly.
Embraced by the dusk's gentle hand,
In nighttime's caress, we learn to stand.

Starry Night's Embrace

A blanket of stars spreads far and wide,
In the tranquil night, where secrets abide.
Each twinkle a story, a wish cast anew,
In the arms of the cosmos, dreams come true.

The constellations weave tales of old,
In whispers of light, their mysteries unfold.
Silver trails dance, a celestial stream,
Guiding our hearts to the edge of a dream.

Beneath this vast dome, we find our place,
In the starry night's warm embrace.
Echoes of laughter drift through the air,
In the night's embrace, we lose all care.

Here in the stillness, our worries disperse,
As we wander through time, the universe.
Each glimmering dot sings of hope and grace,
In the starry night's everlasting embrace.

The Mellow Glow of Dusk

As the sun dips low, the world turns gold,
A brushstroke of warmth as day grows old.
Whispers of twilight begin to arise,
In the mellow glow where serenity lies.

Clouds wear a blush, on the horizon wide,
Painting the sky in hues of pride.
Shadows stretch long, as the light starts to fade,
In this gentle hour, the heart's serenade.

The air feels soft, like a silken sigh,
As the dayfolds gently, we come to rely.
Nature exhales, a sigh of relief,
In the mellow glow of dusk's sweet belief.

Each moment a treasure, as soft colors blend,
In the twilight glow, we find joy to spend.
With every heartbeat, time lightly saunters,
In the mellow dusk, our spirit wanders.

Elysian Fields of Rest

In the valley where soft breezes tease,
A sanctuary calls, inviting peace.
Elysian fields stretch under the sun,
A place for the weary, where all is done.

Butterflies flutter in a dance so light,
Whispers of petals in the warm sunlight.
Nature's embrace in this sacred space,
Cradling the heart in a gentle grace.

Here lies the promise of sweet respite,
In meadows adorned with pure delight.
The world fades away, troubles unweave,
In Elysian fields, we learn to believe.

Let the day dissolve in the horizon's glow,
As stars awaken, their light starts to flow.
In this realm of dreams, the journey begins,
Elysian fields of rest where peace wins.

Starlit Whispers

In the hush of twilight's glow,
Whispers dance on gentle air,
Stars above begin to show,
Secrets woven, soft and rare.

Moonlight bathes the world in silver,
As dreams awaken from their sleep,
Nature's song begins to deliver,
Lullabies in silence deep.

Echoes of the night resound,
Every shadow comes alive,
In this magical surround,
We find the space to thrive.

Hearts entwined beneath the skies,
In the glow of cosmic light,
With every twinkle, love replies,
In starlit whispers of the night.

Lullabies of the Night

Crickets play their softest tune,
Underneath the calming moon,
Waves of peace in night's embrace,
Time slows down, we find our place.

Clouds like pillows in the sky,
Drift along, as dreams float by,
Voices murmur, soft and low,
In the stillness, feelings grow.

Stars provide a twinkling light,
Guiding us through deep of night,
In this moment, let us dream,
As the world begins to gleam.

Hold my hand, feel the serene,
In the dance of night's routine,
Together we will softly sigh,
To lullabies of the night.

Dreamer's Serenade

Close your eyes and drift away,
To a land where shadows play,
In the dreamscape, we shall roam,
In this realm, we find our home.

Whispers echo through the dark,
Painting visions, leaving marks,
Stars align in cosmic grace,
Every heartbeat finds its place.

Time suspends, we float on air,
In the dreams we choose to share,
Melodies of night unfold,
Stories waiting to be told.

In this dance of fate and chance,
All our hopes begin to glance,
With every note, our spirits rise,
In dreamer's serenade, we fly.

Moonlit Melodies

A symphony of silver light,
Plays upon the canvas night,
Each soft note, a gentle kiss,
In the darkness, find your bliss.

Branches sway to nature's song,
Echoing where we belong,
In the quiet, hearts unite,
Bound by moonlit melodies bright.

Step by step, we find our way,
With each moment, come what may,
In this harmony so true,
Magic whispers just for you.

Underneath the endless sky,
Let your spirit learn to fly,
As the stars begin to sway,
In moonlit melodies, we play.

Stars That Sing

In the night sky they gleam,
Whispers of dreams that beam.
Twinkling bright, secrets shared,
Voices of the night, declared.

Melodies of distant lore,
Echoes from the cosmic shore.
Each twinkle holds a story,
In their light, a touch of glory.

Wanderers in velvet dark,
Lighting up the silent park.
Guiding hearts with gentle hums,
Telling tales where starlight comes.

Together they weave a song,
A harmony where souls belong.
Stars that sing, a cosmic dance,
In their glow, we find romance.

Soothing Shadows

In corners where the night falls,
Softly hush the evening calls.
Shadows dance on walls so bare,
Whispers float upon the air.

Nestled in their gentle sway,
Calm the worries of the day.
Cool caress of twilight's hand,
Guiding dreams to peaceful land.

As the world dips out of sight,
Tension fades, replaced by light.
Embrace the stillness, breathe it in,
Soothing shadows, where peace begins.

Beneath the moon's embrace so bright,
Find your solace, pure delight.
Wrapped in calm, let go of fears,
In soothing shadows, lose your tears.

The Art of Restful Journeys

In quiet paths where echoes fade,
Step by step, memories laid.
Each breath taken, heartbeats slow,
A tranquil stream begins to flow.

Gentle whispers guide the way,
Through the night and into day.
The art of stillness, deeply found,
In nature's arms, we are unbound.

Wandering paths of softest hue,
Where burdens lift, and skies are blue.
In restful journeys, we explore,
The peace within, an endless shore.

So take a moment, linger long,
In the silence, find your song.
With every step, let worries cease,
In the art of rest, discover peace.

Melodies of the Quiet Night

The stars hum softly from above,
A gentle rhythm, purest love.
Crickets sing their sweet refrain,
In the stillness, joy remains.

Moonlight spills on dewy grass,
A dance of shadows as we pass.
Nature croons a lullaby,
Underneath the velvet sky.

Whispers of the night unfold,
Stories longing to be told.
In the calm, the heart takes flight,
Swaying with the quiet night.

Embrace the wonder, feel the tune,
Woven softly with the moon.
Melodies of peace ignite,
In the beauty of the night.

Wistful Whispers of the Moon

In the night, soft shadows play,
Whispers of the moonlight sway.
Stars like diamonds, shining bright,
Holding secrets of the night.

Gentle breezes through the trees,
Carrying tales with every ease.
Underneath the silver glow,
Dreams awaken, hopes to sow.

A tranquil heart, a silent sigh,
Beneath the vast and endless sky.
In this moment, time stands still,
As dreams unfold and thoughts fulfill.

Wistful memories in the dark,
Ignite the soul, create a spark.
With every glance, the night enchants,
In the moon's embrace, the heart dances.

Soft Glistening Moments

Morning dew on blades of grass,
In the sunlight, moments pass.
Glistening like tiny gems,
Nature's beauty, pure again.

Whispers of the dawn rise high,
As colors blend and shadows fly.
Birds sing sweetly in the trees,
A symphony of gentle breeze.

With every step, the world awakes,
Soft glistening, all it takes.
Moments kissed by golden rays,
Fill the heart with hope always.

In this dance of light and time,
Life unfolds, a simple rhyme.
Treasured moments, held so dear,
Embrace the day, let go of fear.

Murmurs of a Sleek Night

Beneath a sky of velvet hue,
The night unfolds, serene and new.
Murmurs soft as shadows glide,
In the secrets where dreams abide.

A lone owl calls, a distant sound,
Echoes of peace, all around.
Stars twinkle, a celestial play,
Guiding lost souls on their way.

The moonlit path, a silver sheen,
Illuminates what once was seen.
In the stillness, hearts can breathe,
Finding solace, love believes.

With every rustle, night confides,
In her arms, the world resides.
Murmurs soft, like whispered prayer,
In the dark, find light to share.

The Dance of Day's End

As the sun dips low and slow,
The sky ignites with fiery glow.
Golden hues in twilight's kiss,
A moment wrapped in perfect bliss.

Clouds, they swirl, a canvas wide,
Where day and night can coincide.
Echoes of laughter, fading light,
The day's dance, yielding to night.

With every step, the shadows creep,
Whispers of dreams begin to seep.
A gentle sigh, a final glance,
In the dusk, the starlight's dance.

The night unfurls her velvet cloak,
As hearts awaken, softly spoke.
In this transition, a chance to mend,
Life renews with day's sweet end.

A Lull in the Cosmos

Stars whisper softly, a tranquil show,
Galaxies drift with a gentle glow.
In this stillness, dreams take flight,
Cradled in arms of the endless night.

Planets spin slowly, in quiet grace,
Time wears a veil in this tender space.
Heavenly bodies hum lullabies sweet,
In the vast cradle where silence meets.

Nebulas linger with colors so bright,
Painting the canvas of deep, dark night.
Amidst the stillness, we find our peace,
In the lull of the cosmos, all troubles cease.

Nightbirds and Fading Light

Nightbirds call in the dusky air,
Flapping their wings with a gentle flair.
Fading light wraps the sky in grey,
As shadows dance, beckoning the day.

Whispers of night in the rustling leaves,
Each note a promise that softly weaves.
In twilight's embrace, the world feels right,
As nightbirds sing to the fading light.

The moon peeks shyly through clouds above,
Casting a glow, a soft, tender love.
As darkness deepens, a song takes flight,
Nightbirds awaken in the arms of night.

Twilit Thoughts

In the hush of dusk, the world slows down,
Colors bleeding into a shadowed crown.
Thoughts meander like streams in the mist,
In twilit calm, some moments are kissed.

Dreams flutter softly like leaves in fall,
Carried on whispers, a delicate call.
Each fleeting thought, a flickering flame,
Woven in twilight, never the same.

Here in the gloam where wishes entwine,
Time becomes fluid, like an old vine.
Twilit thoughts dance on the edge of night,
Embracing the fading, embracing the light.

Celestial Driftwood

On shores of wonder where dreams wash ashore,
Celestial driftwood, tales to explore.
Captured in currents of starlit seas,
Carried on waves like whispers in trees.

Fragments of galaxies drift in the sand,
Whispers of cosmos, a magic so grand.
Each piece a story of journeys untold,
Mysteries woven in silver and gold.

The tides roll gently, a lull to the night,
Driftwood glimmers under soft moonlight.
Here we gather, in cosmic embrace,
Finding our place in the vastness of space.

Celestial Lullabies for Wistful Hearts

In the velvet night, dreams take flight,
Stars weave tales, soft and bright.
Gentle winds hum a soothing song,
Cradling hopes that feel so strong.

Moonlit whispers dance on air,
Each heartbeat whispers, 'Do you care?'
In silver beams, wishes ignite,
Known only to the silent night.

Clouds drift slow, like tender sighs,
Beneath the gaze of calm, wise skies.
Each twinkle holds a fleeting prayer,
For lost souls and lovers rare.

Rest, dear heart, let worries cease,
In nocturnal dreams, find your peace.
Close your eyes and drift away,
Let celestial lullabies forever stay.

Glittering Wishes Cradled in Night's Arms

Underneath the shimmering stars,
Dreams ride comets, fly like jars.
In the stillness, wishes bloom,
Echoing softly in the gloam.

Each twinkling light, a tale they share,
Hopeful hearts cast out in prayer.
Cradled close, they twine and weave,
In night's embrace, we dare believe.

Infinite realms where fantasies gleam,
Stars ignite our deepest dream.
Whispers linger in the midnight air,
Glittering wishes, beyond compare.

Hold them tight, as dawn draws near,
Let the magic fill you with cheer.
In silent shadows of the night,
All our dreams shall take to flight.

Dusk's Balmy Breath on Sleeping Eyes

As daylight fades into a sigh,
Dusk descends, a gentle goodbye.
Whispers of night begin to creep,
Lulling the world into soft sleep.

A balmy breath wraps all around,
Tales of twilight weave through the ground.
Silver clouds drift, soft and light,
Bringing calm to anxious night.

The horizon hugs the setting sun,
While gentle shadows start to run.
Hushed secrets stir in twilight's gleam,
As we float through the evening's dream.

Eyes heavy with the weight of stars,
Embracing night's sweet memoirs.
In the cradle of dusk's soft care,
Sleep comes whispering through the air.

Eternal Whispers in the Lap of Night

In night's embrace, a hush untold,
Whispers of eternity unfold.
Flickering flames, softly they dance,
Inviting souls to take a chance.

Stars are keepers of ancient lore,
Echoing dreams from times before.
They twinkling share, in unity bound,
Infinite tales that still resonate sound.

Moonbeams sketch paths on hopes anew,
Each glance a promise, each sigh a clue.
In the lap of night, love's secrets lie,
A symphony soft, beneath the sky.

So gather close, let the whispers flow,
In the night's cradle, let hearts grow.
For in every moment that silence sparks,
Eternal whispers leave gentle marks.

Gentle Glimmers of a Moonlit Dream

Beneath the silver sky so bright,
Whispers of dreams take flight,
Stars twinkle with gentle grace,
In the night's soft, warm embrace.

Echoes of laughter fill the air,
Secrets linger everywhere,
Moonbeams dance on silent streams,
Cradling the world's quiet dreams.

Branches sway in a tender breeze,
Nature hums with gentle ease,
As shadows play along the ground,
In this dreamland, peace is found.

Close your eyes and drift away,
Let the night lead you astray,
For in this realm of silver gleam,
You'll find the heart of every dream.

Stardust Serenade at Dusk

As daylight fades to shades of gold,
The heavens shimmer, stories told,
Stars awaken, one by one,
Singing songs of day spent fun.

Crickets chirp a soothing tune,
While fireflies dance beneath the moon,
Whispers float on twilight's breeze,
Caressing hearts with gentle ease.

Through the trees, dusk's colors blend,
Where shadows stretch and dreams descend,
A tapestry of starry light,
Guiding souls through the velvet night.

Listen closely, can you hear?
The stardust serenade draws near,
In this night, let worries cease,
Embrace the magic, find your peace.

Slumber's Kiss Among the Stars

Close your eyes, the world will fade,
In slumber's kiss, be not afraid,
Among the stars, your spirit soars,
Find solace on celestial shores.

Each twinkling light a gentle guide,
Through endless realms, dreams open wide,
With every breath, let worries cease,
In this cosmos, feel the peace.

The moonlight bathes your weary soul,
Wrapping you whole in its soft glow,
Drifting through galaxies afar,
You are the dreamer, you are a star.

Awake refreshed when night is done,
A brighter dawn has just begun,
With slumber's kiss, you'll find your way,
Into the light of a brand new day.

Night's Embrace and Soft Sighs

In night's embrace, a gentle sigh,
Whispers wrapped in a starry tie,
The world slows down, hearts intertwine,
In twilight's glow, everything's fine.

Each shadow dances, a silent waltz,
Beneath the moon, forget your faults,
Follow the path where dreams ignite,
Lost in the magic of the night.

Soft melodies drift through the trees,
Carried along by a tender breeze,
Every sigh a soft, sweet plea,
To hold this moment, just let it be.

As dawn approaches, hues arise,
Yet in our hearts, the night still lies,
In memory's grasp, we hold so tight,
To night's embrace and soft goodnight.

The hush of Stardust

In twilight's breath, whispers arise,
A tapestry woven with gleaming sighs.
Stars twinkle softly, their stories unfold,
In the hush of celestial, secrets untold.

The universe cradles the dreams we weave,
In moonlit shadows, we dare to believe.
Each glimmering point, a wish made in night,
Guiding our souls with a tender light.

Cosmic ballet in silence persists,
As stardust falls, in gentle twists.
We dance through the cosmos, hand in hand,
Embracing the magic, as one we stand.

The hush of stardust, soft and profound,
In the quiet of night, our hearts intertwined.
Together we'll venture, through darkness, we roam,
Finding our way in the vastness, our home.

The Calm After Sunset

As day gently fades, colors blend,
A canvas of peace, where worries suspend.
Golden horizons kiss the deep blue,
The calm after sunset, a promise so true.

In twilight's embrace, the world holds its breath,
A moment of stillness, a dance with no death.
The chirping of crickets, a soft serenade,
Wrapping the night in sweet, starry shade.

The sky drapes its cloak of indigo grace,
As moonbeams emerge, lighting up space.
A hush falls around, as the day takes its rest,
The calm after sunset, a heart's quiet quest.

Embracing the dusk, we gather our dreams,
In the twilight's glow, everything redeems.
For in the night's peace, our spirits take flight,
The calm after sunset, our beacon of light.

The Gentle Art of Letting Go

In tender moments, we learn to release,
The weight of our fears, seeking inner peace.
Like leaves in the wind, we drift and we sway,
The gentle art of letting go, come what may.

Embracing the change, we find our own way,
In the heart of the storm, we learn to stay.
With every goodbye, a new dawn will rise,
The gentle art of letting go, no disguise.

Memories linger, like shadows in light,
We cherish each moment, knowing it's right.
With grace we move forward, our hearts open wide,
The gentle art of letting go, side by side.

In the ebb and the flow, we discover our soul,
Each end a beginning, as we seek to be whole.
Through love and through loss, we find we can grow,
The gentle art of letting go, the sweetest show.

Fading Light on Soft Pillows

As daylight wanes, shadows start to creep,
Fading light on soft pillows, whispers of sleep.
A cozy embrace where dreams softly flow,
In the twilight's hush, our worries let go.

The gentle caress of night wraps us tight,
In the warmth of our haven, everything feels right.
With eyes gently closing, we drift into air,
Fading light on soft pillows, love's tender care.

In the stillness of night, our hearts intertwine,
As starlit reflections dance through the pine.
A sanctuary found in the depths of the dark,
Fading light on soft pillows, igniting a spark.

So gather your dreams, let your spirit be free,
For tomorrow awaits, with possibilities.
In fading light's glow, let the world softly call,
Fading light on soft pillows, our safe place for all.

The Harmony of Restful Nights

In quiet rooms where shadows play,
The stars above begin to sway.
Whispers of dreams in gentle flight,
Embrace the peace of restful night.

With softest sighs the world will pause,
As moonlight bathes in silver gauze.
Each heartbeat slows, a soothing tune,
In harmony beneath the moon.

The crickets sing their lullaby,
While clouds drift slowly through the sky.
A calm so deep, it wraps the soul,
In restful nights, we find our whole.

Slumber calls with tender grace,
Inviting all to find their place.
In dreams we dance, with spirits light,
In harmony, through restful night.

Drowsy Desires

When twilight spreads its velvet cloak,
And weary hearts begin to soak.
Drowsy wishes softly rise,
Like whispered secrets to the skies.

In twilight's glow, the mind drifts far,
To places where our dreams are stars.
Each thought a petal, sweet and rare,
In gardens made of whispered air.

As eyelids flutter, softly fall,
We hear the night's enchanting call.
Drowsy desires in shadows weave,
A tapestry of what we believe.

With every sigh, the world grows dim,
To dreams of love, we solemnly swim.
In drowsy arms we lay entwined,
In warmth of night, our hearts aligned.

The Secret Garden of Stillness

In corners where the silence grows,
A secret garden gently flows.
With emerald leaves and petals bright,
It welcomes all to seek the light.

Each breath a flower, soft and rare,
In stillness found, beyond compare.
A melody of quiet grace,
Where time forgets to leave a trace.

Amongst the blooms, the heart can mend,
In tranquil moments, find a friend.
With every whisper of the breeze,
The secret garden puts us at ease.

In shadows cast by twilight's hand,
We journey through this wondrous land.
In silent beauty, truth is laid,
In the secret garden, dreams are made.

Echoing Starlight

In the embrace of midnight's breath,
Echoes of starlight conquer death.
Each twinkling light, a story shared,
In the celestial realm, unprepared.

With every sparkle, wishes soar,
On cosmic wings, forever more.
In silent realms where shadows hide,
The universe opens wide.

As time drips down like silver streams,
We catch the echoes of our dreams.
In starlit paths where lovers tread,
Their whispers linger long after bed.

With every heartbeat, stars align,
Echoing love in endless time.
In cosmic dance, we find our place,
In echoing starlight's warm embrace.

Serene Starscape

In the velvet night so deep,
The stars like diamonds softly peep.
Whispers of the night arise,
Painting wonders in the skies.

Moonbeams dance on silver lakes,
A gentle breeze, the silence breaks.
Constellations swirl and twirl,
As dreams unfurl in this bright whirl.

Beneath this vast and tranquil dome,
The universe feels just like home.
Each twinkle tells a tale of old,
In a language soft and bold.

Gazing up with peaceful hearts,
We are all connected parts.
In this starscape, we belong,
Embracing night with whispered song.

Sleepytime Stories of the Night

The moon begins its gentle climb,
Telling tales of olden time.
Softy wrapped in nighttime's grace,
Dreamers drift to a quiet space.

Whispers of the night unfold,
Stories of the brave and bold.
In the hush, a secret sigh,
As shadows dance and dreamers fly.

Lost in lands where fairies play,
Where shadows guide the starry way.
Each story weaves a tender seam,
A lullaby that cradles dream.

Sleepytime whispers warm and light,
Guide us gently through the night.
Wrapped in tales from head to toe,
We find the calm to let dreams flow.

Lullabies Under Starlit Skies

Underneath the starlit glow,
Gentle breezes come and go.
Crickets sing, a soft refrain,
A lullaby across the plain.

Each star twinkles like a sigh,
As the night begins to fly.
Holding dreams in tender care,
A peaceful moment lingers there.

In this quiet, hearts are free,
Swaying softly like the sea.
Every note a sweet embrace,
In the night's harmonious space.

Lullabies will lead us home,
In this realm where dreamers roam.
Underneath the cosmic light,
We drift gently into night.

Dreams in the Whispering Night

In the whispering night we lay,
Chasing shadows, dreams at play.
The stars above begin to gleam,
Woven threads of every dream.

The night enfolds us, soft and wide,
With secrets that the shadows hide.
A canvas painted deep with night,
Where wishes take their graceful flight.

Every heartbeat sings a tune,
Underneath the watchful moon.
Glimmers of what's yet to be,
In the hush, we roam so free.

Dreams in whispers take their course,
Guided by a tranquil force.
With each breath, we drift and sway,
In the magic of the day.

Celestial Cradle of Soft Murmurs

In the night, the stars do whisper,
Gentle secrets of the sky,
A cradle made of soft light,
Where dreams and wishes lie.

Above, the moon glows softly,
Casting beams on silent streams,
The world wrapped in silver silence,
As we drift through tender dreams.

Crickets sing their lullabies,
While shadows dance in the breeze,
Nature cradles our desires,
In this moment, we find peace.

In the heart of night's embrace,
Soft murmurs guide our way,
Celestial whispers interlace,
In twilight's gentle sway.

Radiant Reflections in Velvet Shadows

Underneath the velvet skies,
Reflections twinkle like the stars,
Each moment caught in fleeting light,
Dreams escape to cosmic bars.

The night unfurls its tapestry,
A story woven with twilight threads,
Radiant hues in shadows play,
Where the past and present wed.

Moonlight dances on the lake,
Echoes of laughter linger near,
Soft whispers carried by the breeze,
In this realm, all is clear.

Glistening paths of dreams unfold,
Dancing in the silver glow,
In the embrace of night so bold,
Radiant reflections flow.

Drowsy Dances Beneath Cosmic Dreams

In the stillness, shadows glide,
Dancing softly through the night,
Cosmic dreams in every step,
An ethereal ballet of light.

Stars entwine in harmony,
Each twinkle tells a tale,
Whispers of the galaxy,
On a gentle, cosmic trail.

Beneath the glow of starlit skies,
The universe holds its breath,
For moments lost in slumber's sighs,
Where time dances with a gentle heft.

Floating on the currents of time,
We sway in the night's embrace,
In drowsy dances, all align,
Beneath the cosmos' grace.

Nocturnal Melodies of Fading Light

When daylight fades to softest hue,
Nocturnal whispers take their flight,
Each melody a sweet adieu,
To the warmth of fading light.

As candles flicker, shadows play,
Echoes fill the quiet space,
The nightingale begins to sway,
In this hushed, enchanting place.

Heartbeats pulse in twilight's breath,
While stars awaken one by one,
In melodies we transcend death,
Under the spell of the moon's run.

Songs of night blanket the earth,
With every note, the world ignites,
In the embrace of a soft mirth,
Nocturnal melodies take flight.

Embracing the Night's Glow

Stars sprinkle gold on the dark,
Whispers of moonlight paint the park.
Shadows dance in the tender breeze,
Time slows down, the heart finds ease.

Night wraps its arms around the day,
Sparking dreams that softly sway.
Silent moments, secrets shared,
In twilight's embrace, no soul is scared.

The sky, a canvas, deep and wide,
Crickets serenade with pride.
Each twinkle tells a tale untold,
In night's embrace, our spirits unfold.

Glistening paths in a silver hue,
The world feels fresh, yet old and new.
Embracing night, we drift and roam,
Finding in darkness, a place called home.

Reveries of the Wandering Mind

Thoughts like rivers, flow and sway,
Drifting through night, led astray.
Scenes of wonder, worlds unfold,
Imaginations vibrant and bold.

A whisper here, a shadow there,
Lost in dreams, without a care.
Echoes of laughter, gentle sighs,
In this realm, the spirit flies.

Mountains of memory, valleys of light,
Finding solace in the night.
Every twist and turn a song,
In the dance of the mind, we belong.

In silence, just me and the stars,
Exploring vast and distant bars.
Construction of thoughts, a maze divine,
In reverie, our souls align.

The Sounds of a Sleeping Town

Softly falls the gentle night,
Windows closed, the world feels right.
Hushed whispers in the moonlit air,
Crickets tune their evening prayer.

Doorsteps creak in rhythmic gait,
Peeking shadows, time stands still, fate.
Distant echoes of dreams take flight,
Calm envelops the sleepy night.

A clock ticks down the last of light,
Nature yawns, bids day goodnight.
Silent streets where memories roam,
In this hush, we find our home.

The town breathes in soothing grace,
Every sound holds a remembered face.
As stars twinkle, hearts align,
In the stillness, love will shine.

Dreamscape Delights

In the realm where fantasies play,
Colors blend, and shadows sway.
Floating softly on a whispered breeze,
Lost in wonder, hearts find ease.

Moonlit paths of marshmallow dreams,
Where laughter flows in silvery streams.
Clouds of candy, skies of delight,
Every heartbeat dances with night.

Echoes of joy whisper sweet sounds,
Every corner of magic abounds.
Through this landscape, dreams ignite,
In dreamscape's arms, we take flight.

Wandering free, spirits entwined,
In a world crafted by the mind.
From dawn's embrace to twilight's kiss,
In dreamscape delights, we find our bliss.

Gentle Raindrops on the Windowpane

Gentle raindrops dance and play,
Melodies of the cloudy gray.
They trace their paths with tender grace,
Nature's tears in soft embrace.

Whispers of the evening chill,
A tranquil heart, a peaceful thrill.
Each drop a moment, fleeting, sweet,
A rhythm of the world's heartbeat.

The window frames this soft ballet,
Where dreams drift in the milky way.
With every splash, the silence sings,
A quiet joy that comfort brings.

So let the raindrops gently fall,
In their embrace, I feel it all.
The world outside may dim and fade,
But here, within, the light cascades.

Night's Soft Embrace

As dusk descends, the stars ignite,
A tapestry of dreams in flight.
The moon breathes softly, silver bright,
In night's embrace, the world feels right.

Whispers of shadows softly gleam,
Cradled in a tender dream.
The darkness wraps like velvet tight,
A gentle hush, a starry night.

Through trees that sway in breezy air,
Secrets woven everywhere.
A lullaby of crickets sing,
As slumber's peace begins to spring.

In night's soft arms we find our rest,
In quiet calm, we feel the best.
The world can wait till dawn's first light,
For now, we drift in dreams of night.

Dreamy Reflections

In lakes of silver, dreams unfold,
Mirroring tales both young and old.
Ripples whisper secrets clear,
In every glance, a vision near.

The sky above, a canvas wide,
Holds echoes of the evening tide.
As stars emerge in twilight's glow,
The night reveals what dreams can sow.

Each heartbeat pulses with the stars,
Guided gently from afar.
Reflections weave through time and space,
A dance of hope, a tranquil grace.

With every sigh of night's embrace,
We find our truth in dreams we chase.
In quiet depths of silken streams,
Our hearts are free; we sail on dreams.

Hush of the Evening Sky

The sun dips low, the shadows grow,
As twilight paints the world below.
In stillness, every leaf does sigh,
A gentle hush, the evening sky.

The colors blend in soft delight,
A canvas brushed by fading light.
Crickets chirp a soothing song,
In nature's choir, where hearts belong.

Beneath the stars, the world slows down,
A peaceful cloak, a silken crown.
In quiet moments, dreams arise,
Wrapped in warmth of starry ties.

So let the evening linger long,
In hush of dusk, we find our song.
An echo of what life can be,
In night's embrace, we all are free.

Dreamscapes Wrapped in Silver Light

In twilight's glow, the shadows sway,
A realm where night meets breaking day.
Soft whispers float on silver streams,
In quiet corners, cradled dreams.

The moon bestows her gleaming touch,
On slumbering lands, a gentle clutch.
Starlit paths of quiet grace,
Guide wandering hearts through endless space.

Beneath the veil of shimmering hues,
The world unveils its whispered clues.
Each starlit spark a tale untold,
In cradle' embrace, our dreams unfold.

So linger here in this tender night,
Where everything glows with a silver light.
In dreamscapes spun from tranquil thread,
Awaken softly, where hopes are bred.

Whispers through a Midnight Breeze

A gentle hush, the cool night air,
Carries secrets with a tender care.
The stars, they twinkle, soft and shy,
As dreams take wing beneath the sky.

Each breath we take, a silent song,
In the dark where shadows belong.
Whispers weave through branches high,
Painting tales that glide and fly.

Amidst the night, the world stands still,
As hearts entwine with a timeless will.
Embraced by night, we find our peace,
A moment caught where worries cease.

So let the breeze carry your heart,
Through midnight realms where dreams depart.
In every whisper, find your voice,
In the stillness, let your spirit rejoice.

Luna's Lull around Slumbering Souls

Beneath the moon's soft, silvery gaze,
The world retreats in tranquil haze.
Luna sings a lullaby sweet,
To guide each soul to peaceful sleep.

Her light caresses every seam,
Igniting hope in whispered dreams.
As shadows dance, they softly sway,
Embracing night in gentle play.

In twilight's arms, our worries fade,
While starlit paths, our hearts invade.
So close your eyes, let silence reign,
In Luna's lull, we break the chain.

Awake anew when dawn arrives,
With morning light, our spirit thrives.
In every dream, a world to find,
Wrapped in Luna's love, intertwined.

Celestial Dreams in Gentle Hues

In hues of blue and shades of gold,
Celestial dreams begin to unfold.
A canvas painted with whispered light,
Awakens the magic of the night.

Each star a wish, each glance a prayer,
In skies adorned with dreams laid bare.
Glimmers dance on the edges of sleep,
A promise made to the hearts we keep.

So let your spirit soar through the stars,
Beyond the reach of earthly bars.
In every breath, find joy and delight,
In the tapestry woven, serene and bright.

As dawn approaches, colors merge,
Whispers of night begin to surge.
In gentle hues, the day is born,
A new adventure from dreams reborn.

Nighttime Whirls

Stars begin to spin and twirl,
In a vast and silent whirl.
The moon casts shadows, soft and pale,
As whispers float on night's cool veil.

Dreams come alive in silver light,
Dancing through the starry night.
In the hush, our hearts take flight,
Lost within the moon's delight.

Gentle breezes softly play,
Carrying our fears away.
In this realm where shadows blend,
Time slows down, and dreams extend.

With every twinkle, secrets gleam,
Boundless wishes softly dream.
In nighttime's embrace, love whirls,
A universe where magic unfurls.

Cuddle Up With the Constellations

Lay beneath the heavens wide,
Where constellations gently glide.
Hold me close, let's trace the stars,
And journey far beyond the bars.

Orion guards the midnight sky,
While whispers of the night drift by.
We'll find our place in cosmic rhyme,
Wrapped in love, transcending time.

The Milky Way, a ribbon bright,
Guides our hearts through endless night.
With every shooting star we see,
Wishes bloom like flowers free.

In this haven, dreams take flight,
Cuddle up, it feels so right.
With constellations by our side,
Together, in this dream, we glide.

Moonbeams over Dreamland

Moonbeams dance on crystal streams,
Casting light on hidden dreams.
Every shadow plays a part,
In the tapestry of heart.

Sentinels of night stand tall,
Guarding secrets, one and all.
While soft lullabies gently rise,
Kissing sleep in whispered sighs.

In dreamland's realm of mystic grace,
We wander through an endless space.
Where wishes float on silken threads,
And hope in every heart spreads.

Moonbeams guide our friendly flight,
Through this enchanting, wondrous night.
Together we'll explore and roam,
In dreamland, we have found our home.

The Night's Gentle Embrace

Softly now the night descends,
Wrapping us in silence, friends.
With every twinkle shining bright,
We drift within this starry night.

The cool breeze whispers secrets low,
In this tranquil world, we flow.
Embraced by darkness, fears dissolve,
As hearts entwine and souls evolve.

Underneath the velvet sky,
Time stands still as dreams draw nigh.
In every shadow, possibilities bloom,
In the night's gentle, sweet perfume.

Together we'll face what comes our way,
In this love, we choose to stay.
With every heartbeat, we will trace,
The beauty in the night's embrace.

Quietude Beneath the Moon

In shadows soft, the whispers creep,
The world is hushed, the night is deep.
A silver glow on tranquil streams,
In quietude, we weave our dreams.

The stars above begin to sigh,
As gentle breezes float and fly.
In moonlit grace, our worries cease,
Embracing all, the soul finds peace.

The nightingale sings soft and low,
While secrets in the stillness grow.
In twilight's arms, we find our place,
Beneath the moon's serene embrace.

With every breath, the calm we seek,
In tender moments, hearts can speak.
For in this peace, the night will stay,
Until the dawn brings light of day.

Shimmering Nightfall

When day departs, the colors blend,
A canvas vast where shadows send.
The twilight whispers, softly calls,
As night descends, the magic falls.

The stars ignite, a sparkling show,
While starlit paths entice us slow.
Beneath the sky's celestial dance,
We lose ourselves within a trance.

A tranquil breeze, a gentle sigh,
The world transformed, the spirits fly.
In shimmering hues, the night unfolds,
With tales of wonder, yet untold.

Wrapped in silence, dreams take flight,
In this embrace of soft moonlight.
Together here, we find our way,
In shimmering night, we long to stay.

Restful Rhythms

The waves repeat their sweet refrain,
As thoughts dissolve like drops of rain.
In soothing tones, the night does hum,
Restful rhythms, softly come.

Beneath the stars, we drift and sway,
In harmony, we night and play.
With every sigh, the heart finds rhyme,
In tranquil moments, lost in time.

A lullaby upon the breeze,
As nature sings with such great ease.
In restful tones, we let it be,
A melody of calm and peace.

Through every heartbeat, every sigh,
In restful rhythms, dreams can fly.
The night embraces, holding tight,
As we give in to deep delight.

Endless Horizon of Sleep

The horizon stretches, dark and wide,
Where dreams and whispering shadows bide.
In tender calm, we softly fall,
To endless sleep, the night's sweet call.

With every star, a wish is spun,
As lullabies of night begun.
In gentle waves, the visions flow,
As peace enfolds, our hearts aglow.

The world retreats beyond the view,
In silent depths where dreams come true.
A canvas painted with our hopes,
In endless sleep, the spirit copes.

With every breath, we bid adieu,
To cares that haunt, to doubts that brew.
In slumber's arms, a journey starts,
To endless horizons, hearts like parts.

Milton Keynes UK
Ingram Content Group UK Ltd.
UKHW020937061124
450571UK00019B/80

9 789916 903926